D1495914

CLONING

By Dr. Susan Aldridge

NEW
FOREST
PRESS

Publisher: Melissa Fairley
Art Director: Faith Booker
Editor: Miranda Smith
Designer: Sara Greasley
Production Controller: Ed Green
Production Manager: Suzy Kelly

ISBN: 978-1-84898-326-7
Library of Congress Control Number: 2010925192
Tracking number: nfp0001

North American edition copyright © *TickTock* Entertainment Ltd. 2010
First published in North America in 2010 by *New Forest Press*,
PO Box 784, Mankato, MN 56002
www.newforestpress.com

Printed in the USA
9 8 7 6 5 4 3 2 1

Picture credits (t=top; b=bottom; c=center; OFC= outside front cover; OBC=outside back cover):
Alamy: 24 (Roslin Institute/Phototake). Corbis: 7b (Sunset Boulevard); 43t (YONHAP/epa).
Getty Images: 6t (Derek Bromhall); 46t; 52t; 54t. iStock: 21; 46–47b; 61b. Science Photo Library:
4–5 (Hazel Appleton Centre for Infections/Health Protection Agency); 10t (Laguna Design); 12c (Dr.
Gopal Murti); 14–15 (Juergen Berger); 15t (BSIP, HARDAS); 18–19t (Geoff Kidd); 23t (Dr. Gopal
Murti); 26t (W. A. Ritchie/Roslin Institute/Eurelios); 27b (Hybrid Medical Animation); 28t (Philippe
Plailly/Eurelios); 29t (Mauro Fermariello); 30–31 (Dr. Jeremy Burgess); 34–35 (Steve Allen);
38–39 (Klaus Guldbrandsen); 40t (Pascal Goetgheluck); 41b (Paul Gunning); 42t (James King-
Holmes); 48t (Patrick Landmann); 53t (James King-Holmes); 56–57 (Dr. Gopal Murti);
48t (Ioanis Xynos); 59t. Shutterstock: OFC; OBC (all); 1 (all and throughout); 2, 3
(all and throughout); 8–9; 11–12; 23; 32–33t and b; 34; 36–37; 44–45; 50–51.
Wellcome Images: 20t (Spike Walker)

NOTE TO READERS
The website addresses are correct at the time of publishing. However, due to the ever-changing
nature of the Internet, websites and content may change. Some websites can contain links that are
unsuitable for children. The publisher is not responsible for changes in content or website addresses.
We advise that Internet searches are supervised by an adult.

WHAT IS CLONING?

A CLONE IS A COPY. BIOLOGICALLY, CLONING HAS BEEN HAPPENING IN BACTERIA FOR MANY YEARS. BACTERIA REPRODUCE THEMSELVES IN A VERY SIMPLE WAY BY SPLITTING INTO TWO IDENTICAL HALVES. EACH IS A CLONE OF THE OTHER.

CLONING BACTERIA AND PLANTS

Scientists have exploited this natural process by adding pieces of "foreign" **DNA** to a bacterium and allowing it to reproduce in order to create many copies of the DNA for study.

Plants can be easily cloned , too. Every **cell** of a plant has the ability to create a whole new organism. If people take a cutting—a piece of stalk or a leaf—or even a sample of cells and give it the right growing conditions, a whole new plant can be generated.

CLONING ANIMALS

It has been difficult to clone animals, physically and for ethical reasons. In the 1950s and 1960s, scientists had some success when they tried to clone frogs. Then, in 1984, researchers at the University of Cambridge, U.K., managed to insert a nucleus from an **embryo** of a sheep into an empty egg cell and created an embryo that was a copy, or clone, of the donor. This process revealed something important about animal cells. Although they are not capable, like plant cells, of regenerating a complete organism if left to themselves, they can be manipulated in the laboratory to make them do this.

When Dolly the sheep, created from an adult cell—rather than an embryo cell—was born in 1996 and announced to the world in 1997, it was clear that the stage was set to clone any animal—even a human.

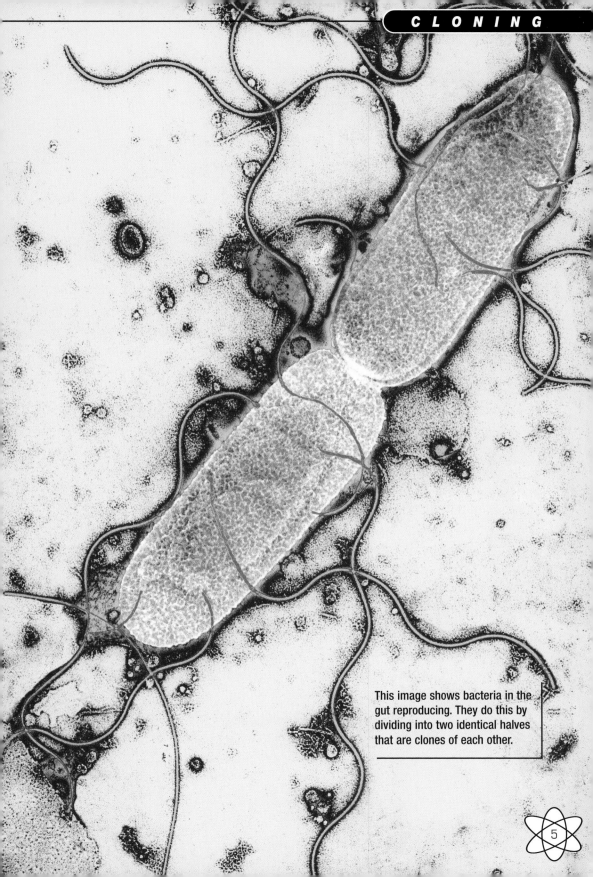

This image shows bacteria in the gut reproducing. They do this by dividing into two identical halves that are clones of each other.

This is a photograph of Dolly when she was a lamb, walking with her mother. The most famous sheep in the world was cloned from part of her mother's mammary gland.

DOLLY THE SHEEP

The birth of Dolly the sheep was announced in 1997, but why had she been created? Scientists had taken a single body cell and created a whole new organism from it. That this could be done at all with an animal was surprising. The process involved reprogramming a cell that seemed "committed" to being part of the animal's udder; this cell reverted to being an embryo. And since sheep are mammals, presumably the same cloning could be repeated in humans.

CONCERNS ABOUT CLONING

Concerns arose because it was obvious that cloning Dolly had been difficult—it took 277 attempts. To try to do the same in humans would surely be unacceptable. Yet it seemed likely that someone would try to achieve this feat. And, if they did, how could the technology be controlled? People might try to clone famous or talented people—even dead individuals. They might try to "photocopy" themselves or recreate dead children or loved ones.

▶▶ www.ehow.com/about_5019077_history-cloning.html

THE BENEFITS OF CLONING

These often-voiced fears conceal the possible benefits of cloning. Maybe the possibility of cloning oneself might sidestep the problems of infertility, where people may not be able to produce their own eggs or sperm. And cloning embryos could supply people with a "spare" kit of cells, without an embryo ever having any possibility of growing into a baby. To assess the rights and wrongs of cloning, it is important to know about the underlying science.

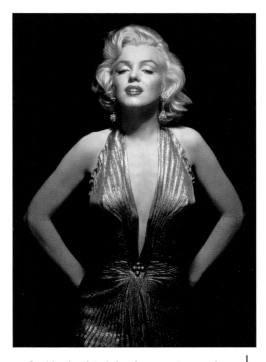

Could scientists bring famous stars such as Marilyn Monroe back to life by cloning?

A CAREER IN SCIENCE

Dr. Steen Willadsen was educated at the Royal Veterinary College of Copenhagen, Denmark, and achieved degrees in veterinary science and reproductive physiology. He became a researcher at the British Agricultural Research Council's Unit on Reproductive Physiology and Biochemistry.

A DAY IN THE LIFE OF . . .

Dr. Willadsen developed a way of freezing, storing, and then thawing out livestock embryos. He also discovered that a jellylike substance called agar protected the embryos so that they could survive the experiments without any damage. These new techniques were essential to the science of cloning and enabled Willadsen to create the first cloned farm animal in 1984. Later, he cloned a cow, and he has also worked on chimeras, combining the cells of different embryos. In this way, he has created animals that have the characteristics of sheep and goats, and sheep and cows.

THE SCIENTIST SAYS . . .

"The role of the scientists is to break the laws of nature rather than to establish, let alone accept, them." Quote taken from *Clone* written by Gina Kolata.

CHAPTER ONE

CELL LIFE

CELLS ARE THE BUILDING BLOCKS OF ALL LIVING THINGS, FROM BACTERIA AND INSECTS TO PLANTS AND HUMAN BEINGS. SOME ORGANISMS, SUCH AS AMOEBAS AND ALL BACTERIA, CONSIST OF ONLY A SINGLE CELL. MORE COMPLEX ORGANISMS, SUCH AS DOGS, HORSES, AND HUMANS, ARE MADE UP OF BILLIONS OF CELLS, ALL WORKING TOGETHER.

SEEING CELLS

Cells are small—the largest cell, the human egg, is only one tenth of a millimeter in diameter. English scientist Robert Hooke (1635–1703) first described cells when he saw them under a **microscope** that he had invented. It was not until the 1800s, with the invention of dyes that could stain cells, that researchers learned more about how cells reproduce themselves.

Today, in hospitals, cells from patients are examined under a microscope by **cytologists** to help in the diagnosis of disease. If someone has a bacterial infection such as pneumonia, samples can be checked to see which species is involved. The result will help a doctor prescribe the right antibiotic drug. Meanwhile, cells can be used in their own right—as a therapy or to manufacture useful products. In blood transfusions, red blood cells are infused into people who have lost blood. White blood cells are used in bone marrow transplants in order to boost the immune systems of people with leukemia.

NEW DISCOVERIES

Cell therapies have been given a boost by the discovery of **stem cells**. These have the potential for repair and **regeneration** of parts of the body that are "broken." Cloning is a way of producing stem cells that can be matched to an individual without the fear of rejection.

The red cells in human blood contain a red pigment, hemoglobin, and transport oxygen around the body. There are fewer white cells, but they play an important part in the immune response of the body.

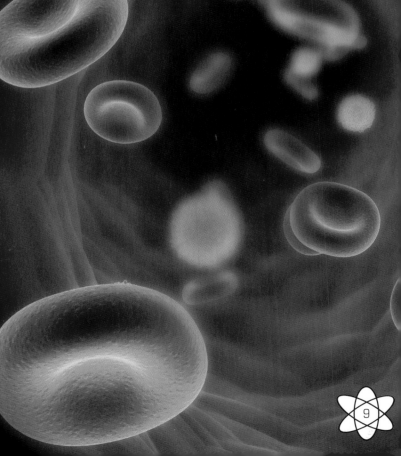

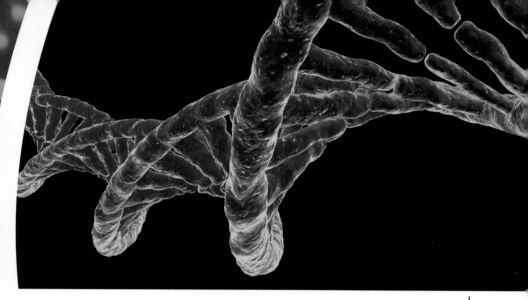

This computer model shows a molecule of DNA, with its two strands twisted into a double helix. DNA contains sections called genes that encode the body's genetic information.

THE WORLD OF THE CELL

A cell is like a factory carrying out many different jobs to keep an organism going. The nucleus issues the commands. The engine room is the **mitochondria**—tiny structures where the cell's fuel (glucose, from food) is turned into energy. The recycling units are found in the lysosomes or peroxisomes, which break down worn-out or damaged enzyme molecules.

UNRAVELING DNA

If you look at a cell under a high-powered microscope, its central nucleus will be clearly visible (except for red blood cells, which do not have a nucleus). There are threadlike structures called **chromosomes** that are made up of the cell's DNA molecule wound around a "scaffold" of **protein** molecules. A DNA molecule is like a very long string of beads, where each bead spells out a letter of chemical code. In humans, this string is almost 6.5 ft. (2m) long, and it is packed into 23 pairs of chromosomes in the nucleus of a cell.

The DNA molecule carries a lot of information in a sequence called the human **genome**, made up of around 30,000 **genes**.

▶▶ www.youtube.com/watch?v=XuUpnAz5y1g

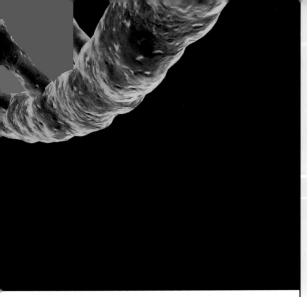

Every gene contains the "recipe" for a protein molecule. Most of the proteins in a cell are **enzymes**. Enzymes in human cells carry out specific jobs—such as breaking down glucose for energy or helping the cells make specific body chemicals, such as melanin, the pigment that gives skin its color.

Genes can be turned on or off. In a brain cell, the melanin gene is turned off, but genes for chemicals called neurotransmitters, which are the brain's messengers, are turned on. Skin cells have the melanin gene turned on but neurotransmitter genes turned off. In short, what distinguishes one type of cell from another is the pattern of "on" and "off" switches along its genome. All cells have a copy of the genome, but the genes within it have a different pattern of activity.

INVESTIGATING THE EVIDENCE: THE HUMAN GENOME PROJECT

The investigation: The main goals of the **Human Genome Project** were to identify all of the genes in human DNA and to determine the sequence of the three billion chemical **base pairs,** or "letters," that make up the human DNA molecule.

The scientists: The project was organized by the United States Department of Energy and the National Institutes of Health. Scientists at the U.K.'s Wellcome Trust and from Japan, France, Germany, and China also worked on the Human Genome Project, making it a truly international effort.

Collecting the evidence: DNA from a pool of human donors was split up into smaller fragments, using enzymes. Automated machines called DNA sequencers were used to figure out the sequence of base pairs in the fragments, and computers were used to match the overlapping ends of the fragments and piece the sequence together.

The conclusion: There are only around 30,000 genes in the human genome, not 100,000 as had been believed. Research on the identity and function of many of these genes continues in the hope of finding new cures for diseases and a better understanding of human biology.

HOW CELLS REPRODUCE

Cells make other cells by splitting in half. This is cloning at its simplest, because the cell copies itself to make another cell just like itself. This remarkable ability allows one bacterium to become two bacteria and the human body to grow bigger and repair itself when it is damaged.

CELL DIVISION

Mitosis, or cell division, is a two-stage process. First, the chromosomes copy one another. This is important, because the chromosomes contain the genetic material — the cell's "blueprint" — in the form of DNA. Then the cell splits in half, carrying a copy of the chromosomes into each cell. In bacteria, mitosis takes place around every 20 minutes, and numbers increase very rapidly in a series of multiples — 1, 2 ,4, 8, 16, 32 — as each one doubles. If this continued unchecked, bacteria would soon take over Earth! But each bacterium is a living organism that needs food and space, so many die from lack of supplies before they can reproduce themselves.

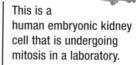

This is a human embryonic kidney cell that is undergoing mitosis in a laboratory.

▶▶ www.youtube.com/watch?v=rgLJrvoX_qo

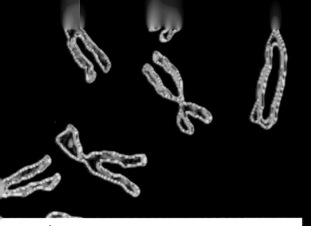

These human chromosomes are each made up of two identical chromatids linked in the center. Some have short arms and some have long arms.

CHANGING CELLS

In other organisms, including humans, mitosis is similar but happens less often—the cells of the stomach lining divide every three days, skin cells every few days, and brain cells hardly ever. Cells divide rapidly when a baby is developing in the womb, but at that time they do not make exact copies of themselves like bacteria. Instead, they **differentiate**—they change from stem cells into more complex cells by turning on various genes within their genome. Ideally, cells that become damaged do not divide and reproduce themselves. Instead, they commit a form of suicide called **apoptosis** that arises from the turning on of certain genes.

A CAREER IN SCIENCE

Dr. Emer Clarke has a degree in biochemistry and a PhD in cell biology from Trinity College, Dublin, Ireland. She has worked in bone marrow transplant research in Seattle, Washington, and then with the U.K.'s National Blood Service. Now she works for a company that supports stem cell research.

A DAY IN THE LIFE OF . . .

Dr. Clarke starts the day by dealing with e-mails —around 40 queries per day from technical staff and customers. Then she spends four or five hours in the laboratory. She needs to report on experiments, count cells, and identify any changes in their shape. The company's products and services help with research in immunology, hematology, and cancer.

THE SCIENTIST SAYS . . .

"I love the diversity of my job. I enjoy going into the laboratory and doing experiments and finding out what's new. There's also the knowledge that the work I do benefits patients. It helps the discovery of new drugs and involves training people in laboratories to treat illnesses."

CELLS, TISSUES, AND ORGANS

The human body is made up of **organs** such as the brain, heart, liver, and stomach. These organs are made of material called tissue that, in turn, is made up of joined-together cells.

MAKING ORGANS

While a bacterium can process food, generate energy, and respond to environmental cues as a single cell, this is simply not possible for more complex organisms. A plant, for instance, has a very obvious structure—roots, stem, leaf, and (maybe) flowers. Its cells must be specialized and work together in different tissues and organs. Most animals and plants are multicellular. Like plants, humans can do a lot more than bacteria. An early human embryo is a ball of similar cells, but a developing fetus and a newborn baby are made up of different types of cells that group together as tissues to form the various organs of the body.

REPAIRING DAMAGE

When a tissue or organ wears out or is damaged, a possible solution is the supply of fresh cells to repair it. The problem is how to obtain these cells and whether they should be used as they are or grown into tissue first. Cloning offers the possibility of creating cells for repair. Skin cells can help heal burns and wounds. Stem cells, taken from early human embryos and bone marrow, can do an even wider range of tasks, such as healing damaged heart tissue or repairing brain disorders.

These stem cells have been taken from umbilical cord blood. They can turn into red blood cells or one of the various types of white blood cells that make up the immune system.

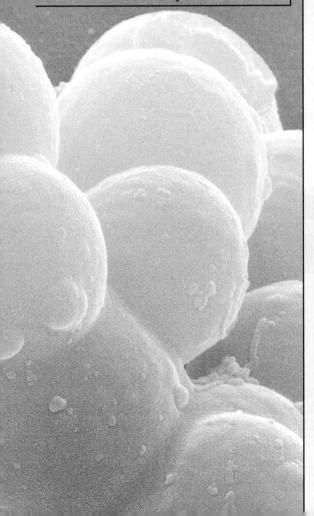

This is an embryo at the earliest stage of development, between 4–48 hours old and only 0.1 millimeter across.

INVESTIGATING THE EVIDENCE: TURNING CORD BLOOD CELLS INTO IMMUNE CELLS

The investigation: Leukemia can be treated with a stem cell transplant, but immune cells called T cells in the transplant may cause an adverse condition called graft-versus-host disease. Other types of immune cells, natural killer (NK) cells, do not have this effect. Therefore, there is a hunt for sources of NK cells for leukemia treatment.

The scientists: Dr. Patrick Zweidler-McKay and his team at the University of Texas MD Anderson Cancer Center in the United States.

Collecting the evidence: NK cells from umbilical cord blood were multiplied 30-fold in a laboratory over a three-week period. They were treated with substances to keep them alive. More than 150 million NK cells were produced from one unit of cord blood. Previous attempts had failed to produce sufficient cells.

The conclusion: The NK cells from cord blood cut the number of circulating cancer cells by 60 to 85 percent in mice with leukemia. The next step is to see if this works in human clinical trials. It is hoped that NK cells can be used in patients without the need for chemotherapy as well and that they could be given to patients who have already had one transplant.

CHAPTER TWO

NATURAL CLONING

ANYONE WHO IS INTERESTED IN GARDENING KNOWS ABOUT CLONING. HE OR SHE CAN MAKE A COPY OF A PLANT BY TAKING A CUTTING SUCH AS A LEAF, TWIG, OR PIECE OF STEM. THE WORD *CLONE* COMES FROM THE GREEK WORD FOR "TWIG." IN THE PROCESS, A "DAUGHTER" IS PRODUCED FROM A SINGLE "PARENT" BY **ASEXUAL REPRODUCTION**. THE REPRODUCTION OF HUMANS AND MANY OTHER ANIMALS IS CALLED **SEXUAL REPRODUCTION**, AND IT INVOLVES THE JOINING TOGETHER OF CELLS FROM TWO PARENTS.

WHAT IS A CLONE?

The word *clone* can refer to the act of creating a new copy of an organism (we cloned this shrub) or it can refer to the copy itself (this palm tree is a clone). The clone is genetically identical to its parent, having the same genes and DNA. The cells of organisms that can be cloned are said to be **totipotent**—each can develop into a whole organism. The cells in organisms that cannot naturally be cloned cannot change in this way.

CREATING TWINS

Human cloning can occur when a **fertilized** egg splits in half to create identical twins. Identical twins have identical DNA, but they may develop in slightly different ways in the womb and so may differ in traits such as appearance or fingerprints. Identical twins are genetically different from their parents. Fraternal twins are formed when a woman produces two eggs that are fertilized by two different sperm. These twins are not clones and share, on average, only 50 percent of their genes. They are no different genetically from brothers and sisters of the same parents born at different times.

Only around one in 250 births produces identical twins.

Here, a gardener is taking a cutting of a well-developed side shoot from a variegated holly bush. The new plant that will grow from this will be a clone of the parent plant.

CLONING PLANTS

Cloning comes naturally to plants. For instance, when a strawberry plant puts out a runner, it takes root nearby and a new plant grows from it. The new plant is a clone of the original. Over thousands of years, farmers and gardeners have invented ways to aid this process.

PROPAGATION

A leaf cutting of a plant has a mass of unspecialized cells called a **callus** at its cut end. When these are placed in soil or a nutrient solution, they quickly multiply into more specialized cells such as root and stem. These cells can grow into a new plant. This is a type of cloning called vegetative **propagation**.

TISSUE CULTURE

Another way of cloning a plant is to take root cells and grow them in a nutrient-rich culture. The cells undergo a process called dedifferentiation, which makes them revert to the callus

▶ ▶ http://mdc.mo.gov/conmag/2001/01/50.htm

stage. If the cells are then exposed to various plant hormones, they will grow into plant clones that are identical to the original plant. This procedure, called **tissue culture** propagation, is used to grow prize orchids and rare flowers.

There is no scientific reason why åall plants should not be grown and regenerated by tissue culture in the future. However, except for rice, cereal plants have proved difficult to grow in this way, which is disappointing from the point of view of increasing the world's food supplies. Tissue culture is low tech, so it can be applied by a wide range of growers. For instance, small-scale farmers in north Vietnam have used tissue culture to regenerate three million potato plants from tissue provided by the International Potato Center in Peru.

INVESTIGATING THE EVIDENCE: MILLENNIUM SEED BANK

The investigation: Up to 100,000 of the world's plant species are threatened with extinction. The Millennium Seed Bank, located in Sussex, U.K., aims to collect seeds—the basic biological materials for cloning—in order to save these precious plants.

The scientists: Researchers at the Royal Botanic Gardens, Kew, and 50 partners around the world. The bank is located at Kew's garden at Wakehurst Place in Sussex.

Collecting the evidence: Seeds come in from around the world and are sorted, cleaned, labeled, and checked to see that they are capable of germination. Most are stored at around −4°F (−20°C). There are many projects under way using the seeds, some of which involve their propagation by cloning. The seed clones can be used for scientific research or to restore damaged habitats. Kew scientists are now undertaking an expedition to the remote Chagos Islands in the Indian Ocean—which have not been visited by botanists for more than 30 years—to see what the conservation needs are and how the bank can help.

The conclusion: The Millennium Seed Bank has already stored more than ten percent of the world's known plant species, and the goal is to increase this to 25 percent by 2020.

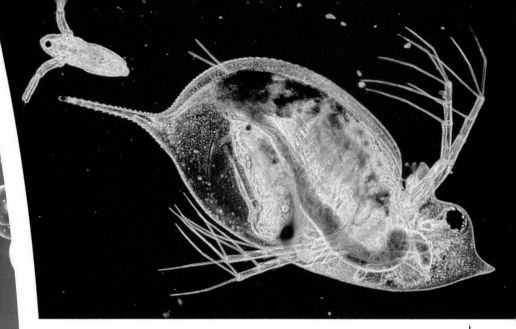

This water flea is giving birth—there is already one young floating free in the water. This is a form of parthenogenesis in which the development of the embryos inside the female water flea has taken place without fertilization by a male.

CLONING ANIMALS

Some animals naturally clone themselves. Experiments have shown that it is possible to split embryos in half and that this results in clones. However, it is sometimes difficult to get a cell to develop into a whole organism.

Since the 1800s, scientists have wondered whether all cells carry the entire "body plan" of an organism. For plants, it looks as if a leaf cell carries a plan and naturally carries it out. However, many animals do not. For example, no one has ever been able to clone a dog using one of its hairs.

PARTHENOGENESIS

The unfertilized eggs of certain animals, including worms, small invertebrates, and some species of fish and lizards, give rise to fully grown animals under certain conditions. This process is called **parthenogenesis**. Experiments have shown that splitting two-cell embryos of sea urchins and salamanders leads to two clones. But researchers wanted to know if "older" cells retained

▶▶ www.youtube.com/watch?v=iiS36VjFrcc

the body plan in this way. In 1962, John Gurdon, a British researcher at the Department of Zoology of the University of Oxford, U.K., managed to clone tadpoles. He did this by inserting a fully grown frog's intestinal cells—the nuclei of which had been destroyed with ultraviolet light—into a frog egg. The tadpoles that resulted did not survive to become adult frogs. However, this first experiment in **nuclear transfer** was to prove very significant for other scientists in the years that followed.

These tadpoles did not survive for long after the first attempt at nuclear transfer in 1962.

INVESTIGATING THE EVIDENCE: NUCLEAR TRANSFER

The investigation: In 1928, the nucleus of the embryo of a salamander was transferred to a cell that did not have a nucleus—the first example of nuclear transfer, the technique that eventually led to Dolly the sheep.

The scientists: German embryologist Hans Spemann and his team of scientists.

Collecting the evidence: Spemann used a strand of hair to force the nucleus to one side of the newly fertilized egg cell. He waited until the nucleus had divided to the 16-cell embryo stage. Then the "noose" was loosened so that the nucleus of one of the embryos rejoined the **cytoplasm**. He tightened it again, breaking off the cytoplasm and the nucleus from the 16-cell embryo. This cell grew into a normal embryo.

The conclusion: This experiment showed that the nucleus from an early embryo cell was able to direct the complete growth of a new salamander. Spemann published his results in his book *Embryonic Development and Induction*, where he writes about the "fantastical experiment" of cloning from differentiated or adult cells.

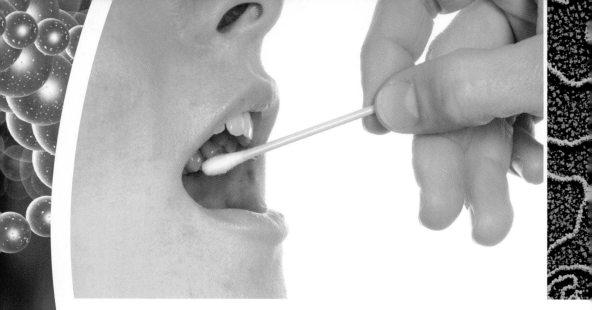

One method of taking a DNA sample is with a buccal swab, which is used to collect cells from the inside of the cheek. Other samples could be hair, skin, or blood.

DNA CLONING

Gene, or DNA, cloning is a technique that has greatly aided scientists in the study of genes. The technique involves using tiny genetic elements called **plasmids** as "vehicles" to transfer a sequence of DNA representing a gene of interest—for example, for building muscle—into a "host" bacterium that will produce many copies, or clones. The researchers then have enough DNA to carry out their experiments. Plasmids are self-replicating pieces of DNA found within the body of a bacterium but are separate from the rest of its DNA. They can be used as **vectors**, types of molecular vehicles.

HOW DNA CLONING WORKS

A DNA fragment containing a gene of interest is pulled out of a bigger piece of DNA. **Cutting enzymes** are mixed with the sample. The DNA is then combined with a plasmid that has been treated with the same cutting enzymes. This means that the DNA and the plasmid come together naturally—scientists talk about "sticky ends" seeking one another. When they join, the result is a **recombinant** DNA molecule, so called because they have combined.

▶▶ http://library.thinkquest.org/J0112600/cloning.htm

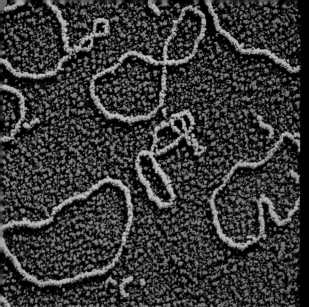

These highly magnified plasmids (yellow) are bacterial DNA from the bacterium E. coli.

INTERPRETING THE EVIDENCE

Plasmids naturally enter into host bacteria, so the recombinant plasmid can become part of a host cell and be reproduced alongside it. A plasmid can carry a sequence of DNA around 20,000 "letters," or base pairs, in length. Bigger vectors include artificial chromosomes based on yeasts and bacteria that will allow larger sections of DNA—up to 45,000 letters—to be cloned. Without DNA cloning, scientists could not have undertaken the Human Genome Project, which has allowed them to map and identify 30,000 genes that make up the human genome (see page 11).

A CAREER IN SCIENCE

Kate Pemberton has a degree in chemistry from the University of Cambridge, U.K., and obtained a PhD in synthetic organic chemistry in London. After postdoctoral research, she did an MA in biotechnology at the University of Hertfordshire. She then joined a Medical Research Council group in London, working on the molecular genetics of blood-clotting proteins.

A DAY IN THE LIFE OF . . .

Some years ago, Pemberton's research group cloned an important blood-clotting protein gene. This has had many spinoffs for Kate's research. She extracts DNA from blood samples given by patients with blood-clotting disorders such as hemophilia and pinpoints the exact mutation causing the disease. This would not be possible without having cloned the gene. Her work is becoming increasingly automated and "high throughput"—which means increasing numbers of blood samples can be analyzed with greater accuracy.

THE SCIENTIST SAYS . . .

"Cloning a gene is the first step in really understanding a disease. Eventually, it may lead to therapies based upon a molecular understanding of the disease. This is more likely to be successful than the 'hit and miss' approach to drug discovery that has been traditionally used. That is why cloning genes is so important."

CHAPTER THREE

24

THE STORY OF DOLLY

IN FEBRUARY 1997, THE ANNOUNCEMENT OF DOLLY THE CLONED SHEEP HIT THE NEWS. HER BIRTH OPENED THE DOOR TO THE CREATION OF CLONED EMBRYOS AND WHOLE ANIMALS THAT MAY HAVE MANY MEDICAL USES. IT ALSO SHOWED THAT THE CELLS OF THE BODY COULD BE REPROGRAMMED TO BECOME MORE PRIMITIVE CELLS.

FIRST SUCCESSES

Researchers at the Roslin Institute near Edinburgh, Scotland, had been trying to clone animals for many years. Their first big success came in 1995, when they announced the birth of the sheep Megan and Morag. Cells were taken from nine-day-old embryos and inserted into two egg cells from which the nuclei had already been removed. The cells divided and developed into two embryos that were placed in the wombs of two other sheep that acted as surrogate mothers, giving birth to Megan and Morag.

A natural next step was to see if the clock could be reversed in adult cells. Three sheep were involved in the creation of Dolly. The egg came from a Scottish Blackface sheep. A sample of cells was taken from the udder of a Finn Dorset ewe. These were given enough nutrients to keep them alive, but not enough to let them grow and divide. One of the cells was then inserted into the egg cell, and a pulse of electric current was applied to it to start the development. The fetus now had nuclear DNA from the donor cell and mitochondrial DNA from the donor egg. The egg was placed into the womb of a third sheep that was Dolly's "mother" in the sense that she carried, nurtured, and gave birth to the developing fetus.

Since Dolly, many other animals have been cloned, including mice, goats, rabbits, cats, and monkeys.

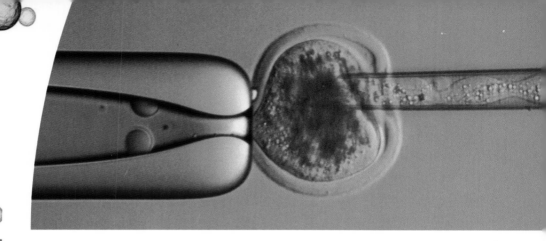

A donor sheep's egg (center) is having its nucleus (DNA) removed from it during sheep cloning. A microneedle will then inject a sheep udder cell into the empty egg cell.

SUCCESS OR FAILURE?

Although cloning a mammal is an impressive scientific feat, it is very difficult. Only a few nuclear transfers result in a live animal being born and surviving to adulthood, and the animals that do survive are often abnormal.

TRY, TRY, AND TRY AGAIN

It took 277 attempts at nuclear transfer before Dolly the sheep was born on July 5, 1996. In animal cloning, only between one and 30 clones are made in every 1,000 tries. The empty egg and the donor cell may not be compatible or the embyro may not divide or develop normally. Implantation of the embryo into the surrogate mother may fail, as may the pregnancy itself.

Dolly gave birth to six healthy lambs that were naturally conceived, but she had arthritis and was overweight. Studies of other animal clones have shown that they are often much bigger than normal, a condition called large offspring syndrome (LOS). Animals with LOS have abnormally large organs, and this leads to breathing, circulation, and other problems. Even without LOS, some clones have brain or kidney problems and damaged immune systems.

These problems are understandable because of what has been done to the donor cell. Its genetic clock is wound back when it is placed inside the empty egg. This puts the donor cell back in the embryo state. But does it develop normally? And do the genes turn on and off at the right times?

HOW OLD WAS DOLLY?

Dolly caught a severe lung infection and was put to sleep in February 2003. The donor cell came from a six-year-old animal, so was Dolly actually six when she was born and 12 when she died? Researchers tried to answer this by looking at telomeres — the tips of chromosomes. These tend to get shorter as cells age. Dolly's telomeres were shorter than expected, suggesting that her cells were aging faster than those of a normal sheep. But the telomeres from other cloned sheep and mice have longer telomeres than expected.

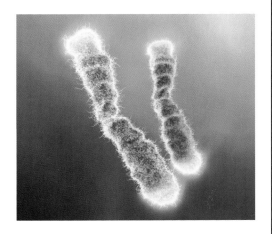

These two chromosomes are highlighted to show where the telomeres are located.

INVESTIGATING THE EVIDENCE: CLONING GOATS

The investigation: Scientists wanted to create goats to be used as bioreactors to produce human therapeutic proteins for their milk.

The scientists: Researchers from Genzyme Transgenics Corporation, a biotechnology company in Massachusetts, Tufts University's Cumming School of Veterinary Medicine in Massachusetts, and Louisiana State University.

Collecting the evidence: The cloned goats were made by taking genetic material from a 40-day-old goat embryo that carried the gene that expressed antithrombin III, a human protein that prevents blood clotting. This was then fused with an empty egg taken from another goat and activated, before being carried to term by a surrogate mother. The team used 285 eggs to produce the three live clones. The first, Mira, was born in October 1998 and the other two, twins also named Mira, one month later. All three animals were fit and healthy.

The conclusion: The three goat clones have produced enough antithrombin III for clinical trials on patients deficient in the protein. The use of animals to make proteins is called pharming and is one of the main applications that is envisaged for cloning.

Second Chance (right), seen here next to its surrogate mother, was the first calf to be cloned from an adult male.

ANIMAL CLONING TODAY

There are now cloned sheep carrying human genes and cloned cattle and racehorses that are copies of valuable animals.

When Dolly the sheep was born, many people worried that the scientists involved were doing it just to show that they could. In fact, the Roslin Institute team had a clear purpose in mind when they cloned Megan, Morag, and Dolly. They were interested in genetically modified, or transgenic, animals carrying human genes that could produce therapeutic proteins in their milk. These proteins could be used as medicines to treat diseases. One of the first proteins they worked on was alpha-1 antitrypsin (AAT), which can be used to stop the destruction of lung tissue through emphysema, a severe and disabling lung disease.

SELECTIVE CLONING

Cloning was seen as a better way of creating transgenic animals. The donor cell would be selected so that it already contained the human gene, which would be more efficient than creating embryos in the hope that they had the gene.

In July 1997, the Roslin team announced the birth of the sheep

▶▶ www.understandinganimalresearch.org.uk/about_research/types_of_animals/animal_cloning

Promotea was the world's first cloned horse and the first to be born from the nuclear donor.

Polly. Each of Polly's cells carried a human gene. In 1998, researchers in Hawaii reported the cloning of 20 female mice. Later, this team cloned male mice using cells from the tips of the tails. They used nuclear microinjection to fuse together the eggs and donor cells.

Scientists at the University of Wisconsin began to use cloning to create herds of elite cattle. The sperm from prize bulls and racehorses has long been used to make sure that animals are born with valuable properties, such as the ability to produce a lot of milk. In 1986, the scientists announced the production of a cloned cow, created using the cells of an early embryo rather than an adult cell.

A CAREER IN SCIENCE

Dr. David Wells has a PhD in the isolation of embryonic stem cells from Roslin Institute in Scotland. He now leads the animal cloning program at Ruakura Research Centre in Hamilton, New Zealand.

A DAY IN THE LIFE OF . . .

Dr. Wells's team is dedicated to using cloning for animal conservation. In 1988, he cloned Lady, the last surviving cow of the Enderby Island cattle breed, the rarest in the world. The clone, Elsie, went on to give birth naturally, and the tiny herd now lives near Christchurch. Dr. Wells's laboratory experiments now aim to better understand how cells are reprogrammed in cloning. He believes that it is faulty reprogramming that is the reason for the inefficiency of animal cloning. The team hopes their research will lead to animal cloning experiments that use fewer eggs than previously and that it will therefore become more acceptable for application in medicine and agriculture.

THE SCIENTIST SAYS . . .

"We need more molecular evidence to determine if there are any longer-term transgenerational effects. . . . We need to improve reprogramming of the donor cell. . . ."

CHAPTER FOUR

GENETIC ENGINEERING

We are all used to the idea of breeding animals for food in the form of milk and meat. Genetic engineering can now create animals that are not found in nature. This is not as unnatural as it sounds, and it could be a useful source of human medicines.

HOW IT WORKS

Genetic engineering involves inserting a "foreign" gene into a host organism. Insulin is a hormone that stores excess glucose (blood sugar) after someone has eaten. It is made by beta cells in the pancreas. Some people are born with beta cells that cannot make insulin, or they become resistant. This condition is called diabetes, and it increases the risk of heart or kidney disease, blindness, and foot amputation. People with diabetes take insulin every day via injection. Insulin was formerly extracted from the pancreases of pigs, but now it can be made by genetic engineering.

Insulin is a peptide—a protein with a relatively short chain of amino acids. Peptides and proteins can both be used as drugs in cases where they are lacking, as in diabetes. However, if they are taken from animal tissue, there is always a danger of contamination. In Great Britain, several people have contracted a fatal disease called Creutzfeldt-Jakob disease (CJD) because they took growth hormone as a treatment for being shorter than average. Unfortunately, the donors had CJD and passed it on through the contaminated growth hormone.

Today, it is possible to use both animals and plants as bioreactors for genetically engineered drugs. For example, sheep embryos are injected with a human gene and grow to produce the corresponding protein drug in their milk.

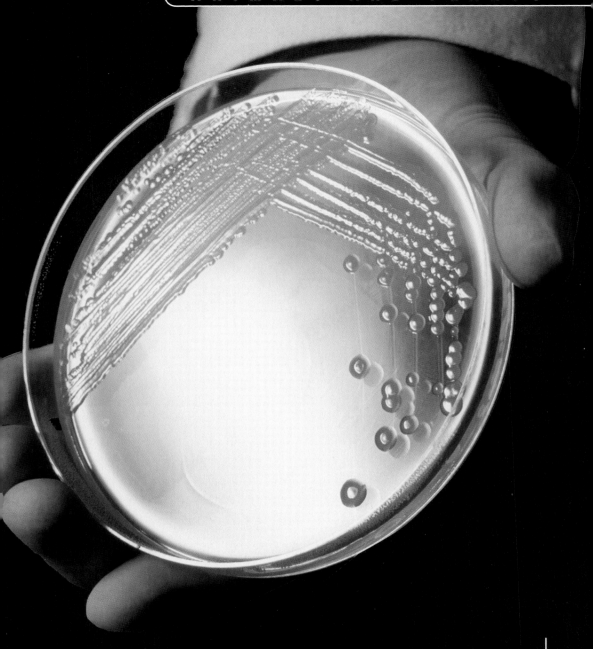

In a lab, insulin is genetically engineered by using E. coli bacteria as a type of factory. First, scientists use a pattern of streaking to isolate single colonies and then single bacteria.

CLONING YOUR PET

If sheep, rabbits, and monkeys can be cloned, why not cats and dogs? Maybe pet owners could store some of their original pets' cells and clone copies when the animals die.

COPYCAT

In 1997, California millionaire John Sperling tried to do just that. He challenged science to clone his dog Missy, and so began the Missyplicity project at Texas A&M University. Unfortunately, Missy died in 2002 and has not been cloned. But the Missyplicity team did manage to clone a cat named

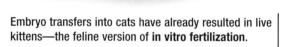

Embryo transfers into cats have already resulted in live kittens—the feline version of **in vitro fertilization**.

Copy Cat. They put what they had learned about pet cloning to use by setting up a company where the public can have tissue samples of their pets banked for use when there has been enough research to making cloning possible. The process is not that different from conventional breeding, where owners truly care about an animal's pedigree.

Many people may be interested in cloning their pet because it is thought that the behavior of a dog or cat is influenced by its genes, and a cloned copy may be similar in personality to the original.

CATS AND DOGS

The company Advanced Cell Technology in the United States has a program that aims to clone cats and dogs—both pets and working animals, including as guide dogs for the blind. The company points out that many guide dogs are neutered at an early age so that they can better concentrate on their work. If a dog turns out to be a good guide, cloning would be one way to make more guide dogs exactly like it.

To carry out pet cloning, the researchers use skin cells from a donor and multiply them to make a cell line—a permanent supply that can be used as donor cells. Then eggs are taken from female animals that have been neutered. It has proved much more difficult to clone dogs than cats, probably because dog eggs take a long time to mature.

INVESTIGATING THE EVIDENCE: SNUPPY THE CLONED DOG

The investigation: The cloning of a dog was done not to help people recreate pets but to advance animal health so that dogs that have diseases may be able to benefit from stem **cell therapy** in the future.

The scientists: Woo-suk Hwang of Seoul National University, South Korea, and his team.

Collecting the evidence: Two eggs were removed from a donor dog's ovary and the DNA removed. A cell nucleus taken from the skin of the ear of an Afghan hound was placed inside the empty egg. The egg was then inserted into a yellow Labrador retriever surrogate mother. Snuppy, the cloned puppy, was delivered by Cesarean section on April 24, 2005. It took 123 attempts with surrogate mothers to create two puppies, one of which died at the age of 22 days.

The conclusion: The more animals that are cloned, the more scientists will understand about the cloning process and the more likely it is to be successful in the future. The cloning of a dog was a milestone in this research.

RARE AND EXTINCT ANIMALS

Reproductive cloning could be used to repopulate the world with rare, endangered, or even extinct species of animals. The cloning of a gaur, an endangered type of wild ox, in 2001 showed that the cloning approach to conservation is a possibility.

SAVING A SPECIES

There are only around 36,000 gaurs left in the world. Their homeland habitats in India, Indochina, and Southeast Asia have been in decline for some years. The cloned gaur, named Noah (after Noah's Ark), lived for only 48 hours before dying of an infection. However, in the same year, a rare wild sheep called a mouflon was cloned, survived, and today lives in a wildlife sanctuary in Sardinia, Italy.

It is hoped that cloning may restore some other rare and endangered species, such as the African bongo antelope, the Sumatran tiger, and the giant panda of China. Success in these experiments depends on a good understanding of how these animals reproduce. There has been some research carried out on embryo transfers of rare species into surrogate mothers.

The gaur is a forest animal that is the biggest and heaviest species of wild cattle. There is a large population in India, and it is sometimes known as the Indian bison.

This young mouflon, or wild sheep, lives at high altitudes in mountainous areas.

INVESTIGATING THE EVIDENCE: BRINGING THE IBEX BACK TO LIFE

The investigation: The Pyrenean ibex was declared extinct in 2000, but scientists had collected skin samples of the last remaining animal, Celia, before she died.

The scientists: Dr. José Folch of the Center of Food Technology and Research of Aragon, Spain, and colleagues from the National Research Institute of Agriculture and Food, Madrid.

Collecting the evidence: DNA from the ibex tissue was inserted into domestic goat eggs in a technique similar to that used to create Dolly. Of 439 embryos created, 57 were implanted into surrogate mother goats. Seven pregnancies resulted, but there was only one live birth. The cloned ibex lived for only seven minutes before dying of breathing difficulties.

The conclusion: A lot has been learned from this experiment, the failure of which may be due to defects in the preserved DNA. Future attempts to revive extinct species may rely on synthetic DNA from the chosen animal's genome.

It is difficult to bring new cherry trees into the U.S. because of quarantine restrictions, so cloning provides an interesting solution to the problem.

POPULAR PLANTS

With all of the discussion about animal cloning, it is easy to forget that cloning plants can be important, too. Plant cloning is successful and is more acceptable to people, because it does not seem to pose any threat to humans. Plant cloning is being used to make plantations of useful trees such as oil palms and sugar maples and to recreate historic trees from plantations that would otherwise die out.

NATURE AND CLONING

Trees are naturally produced from seeds that come from mature trees. Pollen from a "male" tree is blown by the wind to land on and fertilize the ovule from a "female" tree, forming a seed. Then the seed drops from the tree and lands on the ground, where it forms roots and shoots. It will then become a seedling that will form a mature tree over time.

Cloning is a different process. A cutting of a parent tree is taken and may be grafted onto another tree. A small cross or T shape is made, and the cutting is placed inside the cut area and tied into place. It begins to grow, and the growth above the cutting has the characteristics of the first tree. Another method involves placing a cutting into a root solution that contains growth hormones—chemicals that regulate growth. Tissue culture is the most advanced technique of all and involves taking cells from a particular tree and letting each one grow into a clone of the original in a culture solution.

▶ ▶ http://science.howstuffworks.com/genetic-science/cloning1.htm

CHERRY TREE CLONING

These different cloning techniques have been used for a long time and are constantly being improved. Currently, they are being applied to help recreate cherry trees that are being looked after by the United States National Arboretum in Washington, D.C. This is necessary because quarantine restrictions to avoid imported diseases make it difficult to bring replacement cherry trees into the country. Cloning provides a good alternative solution.

A CAREER IN SCIENCE

Minnette Marr is a plant conservationist at the Lady Bird Johnson Wildflower Center at the University of Texas at Austin. She began her career as a high school biology teacher and then obtained a master's degree in biology from Texas State University.

A DAY IN THE LIFE OF . . .

Marr travels for nine months every year, collecting seeds for the Millennium Seed Bank project, in which the Wildflower Center is a partner. She aims to collect between 10,000 and 20,000 seeds for each species. Each collection takes around 40 hours, and she needs several volunteers to help her. So many people are needed because a subsample must be tested on a regular basis over a period of years. Marr travels around the state and has to be very organized to keep up with all of the data that she gathers.

THE SCIENTIST SAYS . . .

"This is not your typical nine-to-five job, where you leave your work behind every day. While the backgrounds of the people I have worked with may all be different, they all have the passion and dedication necessary to work in this field."

CHAPTER FIVE

WHAT IS CELL THERAPY?

THERE HAS BEEN A LOT OF EXCITEMENT OVER THE POSSIBLE USE OF CLONING AS A SOURCE OF CELLS THAT COULD BE USED TO TREAT A WHOLE RANGE OF DISEASES. THIS THERAPEUTIC CLONING MAY, ONE DAY, BE ABLE TO CURE DISORDERS OF THE BRAIN, SUCH AS PARKINSON'S DISEASE AND STROKE, OR HEAL THE DAMAGE CAUSED BY A HEART ATTACK.

A NEW WAY

The human body is a machine in which the working parts—the tissues and organs—break down or get worn out. Medicine has had only two ways of dealing with a malfunctioning body—cutting out the diseased part with surgery or using drugs to try to cure the problem. Cell therapy uses the actual material of the body—cells—to repair, heal, and restore.

GROWING SKIN

The first cell therapy was the use of skin substitutes for treating burns and wounds. Skin is the body's largest organ, and it is composed of the epidermis (outer layer) and dermis (inner layer). The epidermis is made of cells called keratinocytes, while the dermis is composed of **fibroblasts**. It is not possible to create "real" skin in a lab, but substitute epidermis, dermis, and epidermis plus dermis have all been created and are used in hospitals to help patients. The cells are forced to stick together to form tissue by growing them on a biodegradable polymer—a sort of living bandage—that dissolves once it is inside the body. A tiny sample of skin—a biopsy—is treated in the lab to extract the cells, and these are then grown and multiplied in special sterile flasks.

Cells are grown on, and batches mixed with, a polymer to make a sheet of skinlike tissue that can be used to treat a burn or wound.

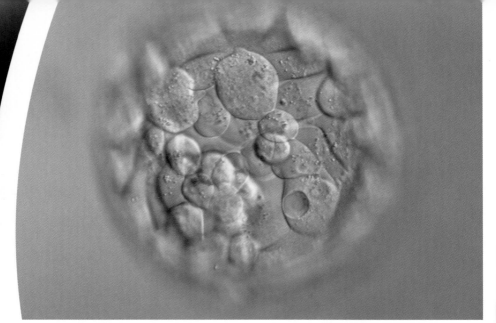

This photograph shows a human embryo at the blastocyst stage. The blastocyst is around four days old and is a hollow ball of multiplying cells.

WHAT ARE STEM CELLS?

For 40 years, bone marrow transplants have been used to treat severe immune disorders and leukemia, a cancer of the blood. Bone marrow is a source of stem cells for blood. Stem cells have two important properties—they can keep on multiplying and they can turn into other, more specialized, types of cells in a process called differentiation.

MAKING TISSUE LAST

A human being starts off as a ball of around 100 cells called a **blastocyst**. Human embryonic stem cells (hESCs) go on to make every tissue in the body. In 1998, only one year after the announcement of Dolly the sheep's birth, a team led by James Thomson at the University of Wisconsin reported the discovery of the first hESC cell line. The cells have been shown to differentiate into neural (brain and nervous system), heart, liver, and blood cells.

There are also stem cells in a developing human fetus—with the period between four and 12 weeks being an especially rich

▶ ▶ http://stemcells.nih.gov/info/basics/

source. Many types of tissue-specific stem cells, such as nerve stem cells, have been found in fetal tissue. For example, fetal cells that produce the brain chemical dopamine can help patients who have Parkinson's disease. Cord stem cells, which are a type of blood stem cell, are found in the umbilical cord and placenta or in a newborn baby. Finally, some parts of the body, such as the bone marrow, skin, liver, and even the brain, have so-called tissue-specific, or adult, stem cells that help renew and replace. Generally, adult stem cells differentiate only into their tissue of origin, although research has shown that bone marrow cells can form other cell types, such as **cartilage** and maybe even heart muscle cells.

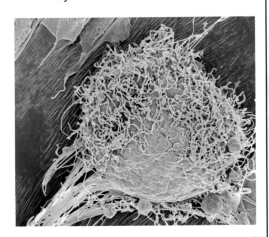

This bone marrow stem cell is from the tissue in the hollow interior of a bone. It can make white and red blood cells and bone cells.

INVESTIGATING THE EVIDENCE: GROWING NEW HAIR FROM CELLS

The investigation: Scientists wanted to establish that **dermal papilla** (DP) cells in the scalp could be used to grow new hair on people who are going bald. This should produce a better result than a hair transplant, where hairs rather than cells are moved from the back to the front of the scalp. Cell therapy should be less painful, too.

The scientists: Dr. Jerry Cooley of the Carolina Dermatology Hair Center, North Carolina, and Dr. Paul Kemp and Dr. Jeffrey Teumer of the U.K. biotechnology company Intercytex.

Collecting the evidence: A biopsy (tissue sample) is taken from a person's scalp. The DP cells are grown in a laboratory and then injected back into the patient using a tiny syringe. The DP cells should grow new hair on the area of scalp where they have been injected. In a clinical trial of seven people, 100 injections, lasting five seconds each, were used to insert DP cells into one square centimeter of scalp.

The conclusion: Hair cell therapy is safe, and five of the seven people (including Dr. Kemp, who took part) grew new hair. The team counted 66 new hairs.

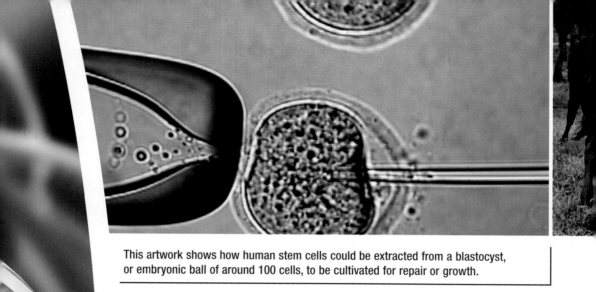

This artwork shows how human stem cells could be extracted from a blastocyst, or embryonic ball of around 100 cells, to be cultivated for repair or growth.

CLONING AND STEM CELLS

In theory, it is possible to bring cloning and stem cells together to create embryos as a source of cells. So far, this has not been done with enough success to be sure of having a good supply of cells for repairing parts of the body. However, if it can be done, the future promise for human health is enormous.

FINDING A SOURCE

Stem cells look like they will be an important source of therapy for regenerative medicine, but there are still problems in finding a reliable

supply. It is a challenge to keep the cells growing in a culture and to make them become the types of cells that are needed. For now, stem cells come from bone marrow and early human embryos that are donated as spares from in vitro fertilization (IVF).

Even if these cells did become available, there could be problems in using them. The immune system of the recipient would treat the donor's cells as foreign and reject them. If the cells came from the patient themselves, rejection should not be a problem.

THERAPEUTIC CLONING

Nuclear transfer of **somatic cells** (NTSC, or therapeutic cloning) could be a way of providing someone with his or her own source of stem cells. This process is theoretical at present

▶▶ www.explorestemcells.co.uk/TherapeuticCloning.htm

This is the first cloned calf created using nuclear transfer of somatic cells in South Korea.

and has not been carried out, but this is how it could work. A body cell of any type would have its nucleus sucked out by a tiny syringe. It would then be added to a donor egg from which the nucleus had been removed. Then an electric current or other stimulus would make the cell begin to divide like an ordinary embryo. The cell would be allowed to divide until there were around 100 cells. Then these stem cells—capable of forming any type of cell in the body—could be grown in a culture. By using the right growth solution, they would differentiate into cells of any tissue that was needed and then collected and stored for therapy. At any time from that point, if the person needed a repair after, say, a heart attack, heart cells with their own personal "signature" would be available.

A CAREER IN SCIENCE

At the age of only nine, Anthony Hollander wrote to the U.K. children's TV show *Blue Peter* about his interest in "making people better." He went on to get a degree in pharmacology at the University of Bath and then a PhD at Bristol University. He worked with tissue-engineering pioneer Professor Robert Langer in the United States, returning to Bristol as a professor, where he is known for his work with stem cells.

A DAY IN THE LIFE OF . . .

Hollander's team made an artificial trachea (windpipe) that saved the life of a young mother of two. They took cells from the bone marrow of Claudia Castillo and transferred them to a donated trachea. The cells and the trachea made a new windpipe. Castillo was the first person ever to be given a whole laboratory-engineered organ. Hollander hopes that this method can be used to create replacements for other damaged organs such as the bladder and bowel. He is also working on a voice box for patients who have lost the ability to speak.

THE SCIENTIST SAYS . . .

"I am delighted that stem cell research has become stem cell medicine. This treatment . . . demonstrates the potential of adult stem cells to save lives."

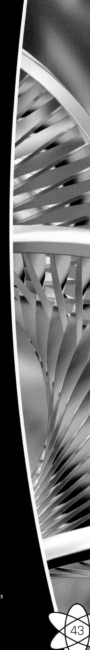

CHAPTER SIX

CLONING HUMAN BEINGS

WITH THE CLONING OF DOLLY THE SHEEP, PEOPLE IMMEDIATELY FEARED THAT THE NEXT STEP WOULD BE CLONING A HUMAN BEING. WHY? BECAUSE IF A NEW ANIMAL COULD BE CLONED USING A CELL FROM A SHEEP'S BODY, IT MUST BE POSSIBLE TO DO THE SAME THING WITH A HUMAN BEING. BUT THE REALITY OF CLONING HUMANS IS VERY DIFFERENT.

CLONING REALITY

Donating a cell would be easy—we have billions of cells to spare. The next stage is to take the nucleus out of this adult cell, which can be done with a miniature syringe and a high-powered microscope. But then the nucleus would have to be put into a human egg (**oocyte**). Women who donate eggs must take drugs to stimulate their ovaries, the glands that produce eggs. And the eggs are retrieved using a type of surgery that can cause discomfort. The nucleus of the egg would be removed, leaving behind just the cell's cytoplasm. Then the donor nucleus would be transferred into the empty egg cell.

There would be two possible fates for a cloned human embryo. First, the cells could be grown to act as a kind of "repair kit" for the body. Second, to grow into a baby, the cloned embryo would need to be transferred to the womb of a surrogate mother, to be born in the usual way. It is possible that human cloning has already been achieved or will be in the near future.

Do we want a world in which people look and behave exactly alike?

IVF BABIES

Baby Louise Brown was the world's first IVF baby, born in the U.K. in 1978. Today, thousands of children around the world have been born in this way. They are often called test-tube babies—but they are not developed in test tubes. Oocytes are collected from the mother and are mixed with a sample of sperm from the father. If all goes well, an embryo forms just as it would if it were

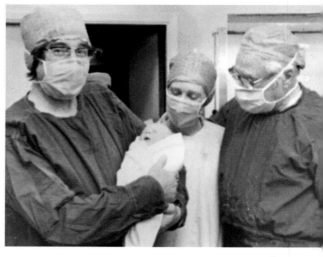

The team that pioneered in vitro fertilization with the world's first test-tube baby, Louise Joy Brown, who was born in Lancashire, U.K., on July 25, 1978

naturally conceived. After up to six days of development, the embryo is placed back in the mother's womb, where, hopefully, it implants and a normal pregnancy is established. It is usual to place more than one embryo back in the womb because this increases the chances of at least one developing.

IVF AND RESEARCH

IVF has been important to cloning and cell research in many ways. It has given scientists experience in handling delicate embryos and an understanding of what happens in the early days of life. Also, there are often "spare" embryos left over

If more than one embryo develops in the womb after IVF, the woman will give birth to twins, triplets, or more.

from IVF because they are not all put back in the womb. A couple could choose to use a frozen embryo in a future IVF attempt if it did not work the first time around. Or they could choose to donate the embryros for research. Embryos (but not eggs) can be frozen for later use and are a rich source of stem cells.

REPRODUCTIVE CLONING

Reproductive cloning differs from IVF in that no sperm is used. An IVF baby has genes from its mother and father. A clone has genes only from the donor and has only one parent. Sometimes, couples have to use donor eggs or sperm because they are infertile and cannot produce any themselves. Instead of looking for a donor who is not related to them, they may think that cloning is a better option for fertility treatment, because it uses one of their own cells (from either parent), and the child will have their genes.

A CAREER IN SCIENCE

Nicola Townsend is an embryologist at the Herts and Essex Fertility Centre in the U.K. She has a degree in medical science and trained in clinical embryology at Homerton University Hospital, London. She is registered to carry out the latest IVF techniques.

A DAY IN THE LIFE OF . . .

An embryologist can expect a diverse routine, involving laboratory work, paperwork, and patient contact. In the laboratory, Nicola and her colleagues work in four main areas: sperm, egg retrieval and fertilization, embryo culture, and embryo preservation. An embryologist needs to pay attention to detail and must have excellent hand-to-eye coordination in order to manipulate embryos that are only the width of a human hair with a small glass pipette.

THE SCIENTIST SAYS . . .

"After my degree, I wanted to pursue a career in the health-care industry but did not want to be locked away in a laboratory. Embryology was the perfect choice, enabling me to combine laboratory work with daily patient care and contact, and has led to a rewarding and fulfilling career."

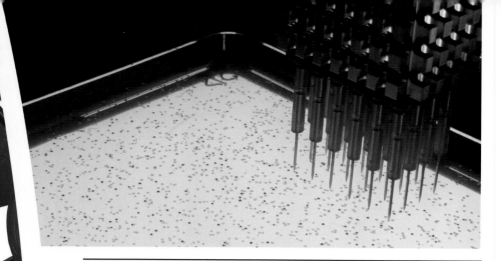

A genetic cloning robot extracts bacteria colonies (black spots)
that have been engineered to contain human DNA for genetic research.

WHY CLONE HUMANS?

Although human cloning is very difficult to achieve, there are several
reasons why people are interested in trying to make it work. It
is important to make a distinction between therapeutic and
reproductive cloning when considering possible applications.

Stem cells are already showing some promise as a "repair kit"
for the body. The problem is that introducing anything "foreign"
into the body—whether it is a kidney or bone marrow transplant,
bacteria, viruses, or stem cells—causes the immune system to
set up a rejection process. This is a way of protecting the body.

HEALING YOURSELF

If stem cells could be made from your own body tissue, the
immune system would not treat them as foreign. You could
clone an embryo from one of your own body cells to act as a
source of stem cells for when you need them. For some people,
this idea of "the clone in the closet" is difficult to consider. But
for those who suffer from a severe disease who may find a cure
through cell therapy in the future, the idea of growing new tissue
from their own body cells is perhaps not so difficult to accept.

There are other possible reasons why people may be interested
in making clones. Sir Ian Wilmut, the scientist who led the team that

cloned Dolly the sheep, was contacted by several grieving parents in the months that followed the press release. They thought he could clone replacements for their dead children, but Professor Wilmut has always said that he has no interest in human reproductive cloning and does not believe it would be right. People may also want to make a clone of themselves simply out of curiosity. But the clone may not be like the original. It could develop in the womb of a different woman or be brought up by different parents and in a different environment. Even its genes would not be completely the same, because they would have that extra bit of mitochondrial DNA from the donor egg. A clone created from an adult would probably be less similar than an identical twin. And even identical twins do not have identical genes. Genes are important, but so are upbringing and environment.

FUTURE FEARS

There are also more bizarre—and frightening—reasons for cloning humans. Powerful politicians or businesspeople could try to clone obedient workers or disciplined soldiers. Or perhaps someone will try to use some preserved cells as donors to recreate famous people.

INVESTIGATING THE EVIDENCE: REPAIRING THE HEART

The investigation: Patients who suffer from heart failure, a condition where the heart is too weak to work properly, are being injected with stem cells to see if the damaged hearts can be repaired.

The scientists: Dr. Anthony Mathur and his team at Barts and The London Heart Attack Centre, U.K.

Collecting the evidence: So far, around 90 patients are being screened at the clinic. They receive an injection of stem cells (or a placebo) into their coronary arteries or directly into the heart muscle. The stem cells are taken from bone marrow from a patient's hip. He or she has a heart ultrasound (echocardiogram) after a few months to see if the stem cells have improved the heart's function. For a patient with heart failure, improved efficiency of the heart muscle means that they are less tired and more able to do everyday things.

The conclusion: The researchers have results from 58 of their patients and are analyzing these to see if there is any real difference between the stem cell and placebo groups.

CHAPTER SEVEN

AN ETHICAL DEBATE

MOST PEOPLE HAVE A CODE OF RIGHT AND WRONG. THIS CODE CAN BE EXTENDED TO SOCIETY, AND GOVERNMENTS BASE THEIR LAWS ON WHAT THEY THINK ARE THE ETHICAL VALUES OF PEOPLE. MANY SCIENTIFIC ADVANCES—ESPECIALLY MEDICAL ONES—CHALLENGE OUR ETHICAL CODE.

FOR AND AGAINST

The potential benefits of cloning include new medical treatments through the therapeutic and reproductive cloning of animals. Cloned animals can be used as a source of organs for transplants. Reproductive human cloning could help infertile couples, especially if it were made more efficient than IVF.

The experience with cloning animals has raised animal welfare concern because many cloned animals are abnormal and have shorter life spans. For some people, therapeutic cloning is unacceptable, whatever benefits it brings, because it "photocopies" humans, and this reduces us to mere machines being turned out by a factory. And what

would it feel like to be a clone? Most humans in that position would probably hate being regarded as a "freak." The alternative would be to live a life of secrecy and anonymity.

IS IT WRONG?

It is often said that cloning is wrong because it is unnatural. But organ transplants and IVF were thought to be unnatural when they were first introduced, and many of the same arguments now being used against cloning were put forward. Today, most people accept transplantation and assisted reproduction. In one sense, there is something unnatural about all scientific advances because they always involve something new and unfamiliar.

Cloned animals have been created in the interests of research, and in time, some benefit may come to humans. But it is difficult to see, at present, how cloning benefits the animals themselves.

51

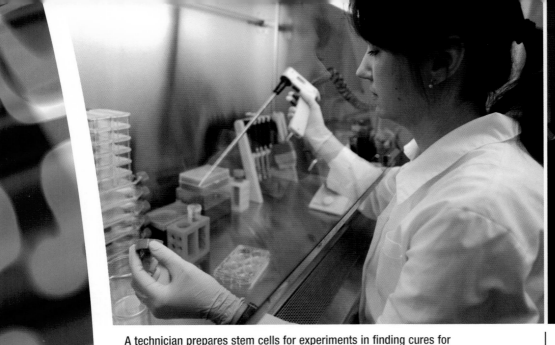

A technician prepares stem cells for experiments in finding cures for neurological and muscular diseases at the University of Wisconsin-Madison.

CLONING, MONEY, AND THE LAW

Public opinion plays some part in how, and if, scientific research is done. A government can control certain scientific activities, such as animal testing, through laws. It also hands out public money for research. When research reaches a later stage, however, scientists usually depend on banks and other investors to fund their work. If the research is controversial, they may not get the money they need to push it forward.

FINDING FUNDING

Science involves much more than the research that is done in a laboratory. If a new medical treatment involving stem cells is the goal,tests will have to be done first on animals and then on people. This is very expensive. When news of a new experiment, promising a cure for cancer or some other disease, gets out, patients often contact the scientists involved demanding to be treated. Usually, that is simply not possible. It can take several years to get a drug or other treatment from a laboratory to a patient. It would be unethical to give a new treatment to someone without

Stem cell research, such as this experiment using a mouse egg, can cause heated ethical debate.

this research because the drug may not work or it may even cause harm.

To get a new treatment to the stage where a patient can benefit, scientists need money to pay themselves, buy equipment, and fund tests. To get a treatment beyond the experimental stage, scientists need money from private investors. And because of the technical and scientific barriers to cloning and cell therapies, it has been difficult to get these people to part with money up front in the hope of a later return. So it may be that people will never see the benefits of cloning because there will not be enough money given to turn the research into a reality.

INVESTIGATING THE EVIDENCE: DISCOVERY OF IPSCS

The investigation: The ethical objections to the use of human embryonic stem cells may be overcome by using induced pluripotent stem cells (iPSCs).

The scientists: George Daley and his team at the Harvard Stem Cell Institute, Children's Hospital Boston, the Dana-Farber Cancer Institute, Harvard Medical School, and Brigham and Women's Hospital, all in Massachusetts.

Collecting the evidence: Four genes were packed into a virus that was used to infect human skin cells. The genes reprogrammed the mature skin cells back to a more primitive pluripotent stage. These iPSCs were grown to become different types of cells. This combination of genes is known to cause cancer in mice, so more work is needed before they can be used in treatments. But iPSCs are already being made into cell lines to study the biology of certain diseases.

The conclusion: We do not yet know whether iPSCs will actually be useful for medical applications. Scientists are continuing to develop iPSC cell lines.

In March 2009, U.S. President Barack Obama, surrounded by stem cell research supporters, signed an executive order reversing the U.S. government ban on funding the research.

CLONING AROUND THE WORLD

There is universal condemnation of human reproductive cloning but a range of different views on therapeutic cloning. For cloning and stem cell scientists, this means that they must pick and choose when it comes to finding a laboratory in which to work. It also means that there are some places in the world where it would be possible to create a human clone—not because a particular government backs it (no country does) but because they do not have a law that bans it.

CONTROLLING CLONING

Cloning is an area of science that governments think should be controlled by the law, mostly in order to stop reproductive cloning from getting out of control. Governments have concerns about three different cloning techniques. First, they are looking at embryonic stem cells, although these are not necessarily produced by cloning. The problem is that embryos are involved, and some people object to this because an embryo has the potential to become a future human being. Second, there are worries that therapeutic cloning may lead, inevitably, to reproductive cloning. And, finally, no one wants to see reproductive human cloning—at least, not at the moment, when it is not even known if it is possible.

This has led to a patchwork of laws around the world. There is no international accord via the United Nations (UN) organization, nor can the European Union (EU), which now covers 27 countries, come to any agreement. In 2001, the U.K. introduced laws banning reproductive cloning. But they do allow work on both human embryonic stem cells (hESCs) and therapeutic cloning.

WEST AND EAST

In the United States, there are restrictions on working with hESCs, and the legality of therapeutic cloning varies from state to state. China is the most liberal country when it comes to cloning. It is behind embryo research and therapeutic cloning, and there is a similar attitude in Singapore and South Korea. In 2004, South Korean researchers announced the production of hESCs from cloning. Since then, the work has been shown to have been mistaken, so we cannot rely on these reports.

INVESTIGATING THE EVIDENCE: STEM CELL TOURISM

The investigation: Since the rules on cloning and stem cells vary so widely around the world, it may be possible to obtain treatments in one country that are not available in another.

The scientists: Doctors at Zheijiang Xiaoshan Hospital, Hangzhou, China.

Gathering the evidence: Two-year-old Joshua Clark from Wales had an undeveloped optic nerve. He traveled with his family to China to receive injections of stem cells from an umbilical cord over a 40-day period in order to restore the optic nerve. Similar operations on two young girls from Northern Ireland have been successful. The Chinese Ministry of Health allows the use of stem cells for many other disorders, including multiple sclerosis (MS) and Parkinson's disease. This liberal law attracts hundreds of patients to China from the West, where such operations are not yet allowed, in particular those who have tried—and failed—more conventional treatments.

The conclusion: Researchers would like to see more evidence that the Chinese stem cell treatments really do work. But it may not be long before such treatments are being offered in the U.S. and Europe.

CHAPTER EIGHT

CELL THERAPY SHOWS THE WAY

THE BENEFITS OF HUMAN THERAPEUTIC CLONING ARE PROBABLY A LONG WAY OFF. HOWEVER, RESEARCH IS BEING CARRIED OUT INTO CELL THERAPY USING OTHER TYPES OF STEM CELLS. IF, AND WHEN, STEM CELLS BECOME AVAILABLE FROM CLONING, THEY WILL BE USED IN A SIMILAR WAY.

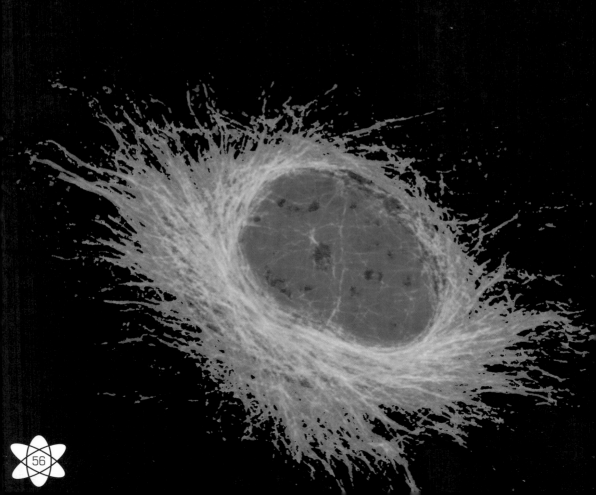

TODAY'S TREATMENTS

Scientists in the United States will soon transplant neural stem cells that they have developed in their laboratories into the brains of children with Batten disease, a rare inherited brain disorder. This will be the first time that stem cells have ever been used in the brain. The results will help advance similar treatments for people with Parkinson's and Alzheimer's diseases and stroke victims.

Cell therapies based on fibroblasts, cells that produce collagen (which gives skin its elasticity), can take an active part in healing wounds, ulcers, and severe burns. Thousands of patients have already benefited from fibroblast therapy. And, for people who want to change their appearance, the cells can also help fill in wrinkles and scars.

Meanwhile, the dermal papilla (hair-producing) cells of the scalp can be grown in a laboratory and implanted on the heads of people who are going bald. This new treatment is being tested in the U.K., and some of the people involved are already growing new hair (see page 41).

STEM CELL BREAKTHROUGH

Bone marrow transplants have long been used to treat severe immune disorders and cancer, but now it seems that these important stem cells can play another role in the body. Clinical trials in Germany and the U.K. have shown that a patient's own bone marrow stem cells can repair heart muscle damaged by heart disease. And it looks as if cells really can be made into tissues and organs. Anthony Atala, now of Wake Forest University in North Carolina, has been working since 1990 on bladders grown in a laboratory from a patient's own bladder cells seeded onto a biodegradable support. The first bladder was transplanted in 1999, and there are reports on the long-term success of the new bladders in young people suffering from congenital bladder defects.

This image shows a fibroblast cell with the nucleus stained blue. Fibroblasts play a critical role in the healing of wounds, and scientists use mouse embryonic fibroblasts in human embryonic stem cell research.

57

In bone implant research, human bone cells are grown in a culture. They are used to develop liquid implants that will form strong new tissues to inject into patients.

THE PROMISE OF CELL THERAPY

The mechanical parts of the body—bones and joints—are prone to wear and tear. Replacing or repairing them with pins and plates is limited. Cells can stimulate a broken or worn area to heal itself by generating new cells. Worn-out knee and hip joints can be helped by using bone marrow stem cells as a source of chondrocytes—cells that compose the main part of cushioning cartilage. The cells stimulate the formation of new cartilage tissue. Bone marrow stem cells can also produce bone cells. In a world first, Australian researchers gave a bone cell transplant to a 21-year-old man with a nonhealing bone fracture. The fracture had been held together with a large titanium plate, and the only other treatment option was a bone graft. The cells were obtained by culturing the patient's own bone marrow cells.

STEM CELLS AND DIABETES

One of the big hopes for stem cells is that they may help heal diabetes, a condition that affects around six percent of the world's population and is on the rise. There are two types of diabetes—type 1 and type 2. The first occurs because the cells that produce insulin

▶ ▶ http://singularityhub.com/2009/04/20/are-stem-cells-on-a-path-to-cure-type-i-diabetes

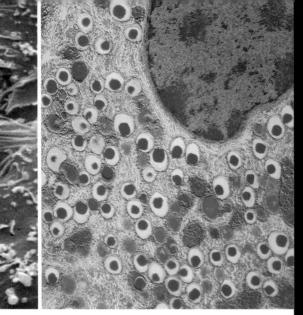

The islets of Langerhans secrete insulin into the blood to control blood sugar levels.

in the pancreas—known as beta cells—are either absent or do not work properly. Transplantation of islets (groups of beta cells) is already an established treatment for diabetes, but the treatment is limited by the supply of donor tissue. Implants of beta cells may provide a better cure.

THE IMMUNE SYSTEM

Tens of thousands of patients with congenital immune disorders or leukemia have received lifesaving bone marrow transplants. The stem cells replenish the blood supply. A bone marrow transplant can also help cancer patients whose bone marrow has been damaged by chemotherapy treatment.

A CAREER IN SCIENCE

Julie Daniels received her undergraduate degree in microbiology and a PhD in tissue engineering from the University of Leeds in the U.K. In 1996, she joined the UCL Institute of Ophthalmology in London and is now the director of Moorfields Eye Hospital's Cells for Sight tissue bank.

A DAY IN THE LIFE OF . . .

Daniels' team works with stem cells from tissue donors, growing them under carefully controlled conditions in a lab. These so-called limbal stem cells are being transplanted into patients who have lost their sight through aniridia, a rare genetic condition, or from chemical accidents. Their limbal cells, under the eyelid, are damaged, and the cornea clouds over, leading to vision loss. The eyes are also very painful. Replacing the limbal cells makes the cornea clear again and restores vision. So far, six out of ten patients given the stem cells in the first trial have recovered their vision, and several more are waiting to be assessed.

THE SCIENTIST SAYS . . .

"Before the surgery, the patients were barely able to recognize when someone was waving a hand in front of their face. We have restored their vision to the point that they can read three to four lines down the eye chart."

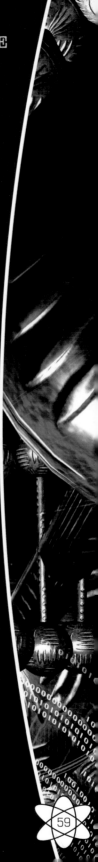

THE FUTURE OF CLONING

It is remarkable that cells can be reprogrammed. Cloning is a milestone in biology research, and it offers all kinds of possibilities. However, such treatments for human diseases are still a long way off, and most people do not want cloning technology being used to create copies of human beings.

A DIFFICULT PROCESS

Scientists recognize that there are many problems involved in working with cells. The process of cloning itself is tricky because it involves the extraction of a nucleus from one cell, removing a nucleus from another cell, and then making a transfer. Once stem cells have been obtained, they have to be kept alive so that they can reproduce, and then they have to be coaxed into making the cell that is wanted—be it a brain, heart, or pancreas cell. When it comes to using stem cells for therapy, there is a lot to learn from using ordinary body cells, such as fibroblasts, which can be used to repair skin and hair. The more we understand cells in general, how to grow them, and how they behave, the more successful all cell therapies will be.

TODAY AND TOMORROW

Stem cells can come from many sources—bone marrow and other "adult" sources, fetuses, and embryos—although it is thought that embryos are the best source. Cloning by nuclear transfer is just one way of making stem cells; the other major source is therapeutic cloning using donated embryos from IVF. But there are other uses for cloning—animal cloning to make a flock of transgenic animals that in turn can be used both for therapeutic cloning and human reproductive cloning. Human reproductive cloning could reproduce humans from a single cell of a donor's body. Whether or not this ever turns out to have a practical use remains to be seen.

These cloned men in the desert are just science fiction—for now! But, one day, maybe such multiple copies will be created as the science of cloning advances. Society must decide if this is right or wrong.

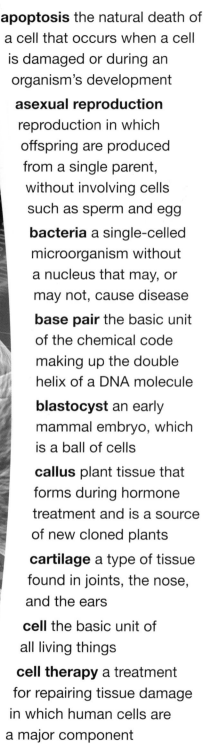

apoptosis the natural death of a cell that occurs when a cell is damaged or during an organism's development

asexual reproduction reproduction in which offspring are produced from a single parent, without involving cells such as sperm and egg

bacteria a single-celled microorganism without a nucleus that may, or may not, cause disease

base pair the basic unit of the chemical code making up the double helix of a DNA molecule

blastocyst an early mammal embryo, which is a ball of cells

callus plant tissue that forms during hormone treatment and is a source of new cloned plants

cartilage a type of tissue found in joints, the nose, and the ears

cell the basic unit of all living things

cell therapy a treatment for repairing tissue damage in which human cells are a major component

chromosome a threadlike structure in the nucleus of a cell that is made up of DNA and protein

cutting enzyme a molecule that can be used to chop DNA into fragments

cytologist a scientist who specializes in the study of cells

cytoplasm the material that surrounds the nucleus of a cell

dermal papilla a type of skin cell that produces hair

differentiate to turn a stem cell into a more specialized cell such as a nerve cell

DNA deoxyribonucleic acid—the chemical that makes up genes

embryo an animal at the earliest stage of development, when the fertilized egg has started to divide

enzyme a protein molecule that speeds up biochemical reactions such as the digestion of food

fertilized describes an egg cell that has united with a sperm cell and that can go on to form an embryo

fibroblast a type of cell that produces fibers and that is found in connective tissue such as cartilage

gene a chemical unit, made of DNA, that carries hereditary information in the form of a chemical code

genome the sum of all of the genes found in a set of chromosomes

Human Genome Project the international scientific project that "mapped" all of the human genes and the sequence of human DNA

in vitro fertilization the process of bringing together a sperm and an egg in a glass dish, outside the body, to create an embryo

microscope an optical instrument that allows scientists to see objects that are invisible to the human eye

mitochondrion a structure within a cell that produces biochemical energy from glucose (sugar) (plural: mitochondria)

mitosis the splitting of the nucleus of a cell to form two new cells whose nuclei have the same number and type of chromosomes as the original

nuclear transfer the process of transferring the nucleus of a cell into an empty egg to create an embryo that is a clone of the original cell

oocyte an egg cell

organ a collection of tissues that carries out a specific function in the body

parthenogenesis the development of an organism from an unfertilized egg

plasmid a structure in bacterial cells that consists of DNA and that can exist and replicate separately from a bacterial chromosome

propagation a form of asexual reproduction in plants where new plants arise from structures such as runners or bulbs

protein a type of organic molecule containing carbon, hydrogen, oxygen, nitrogen, and sulfur; proteins are found in all living organisms

recombinant containing genes from different organisms combined by genetic engineering

regeneration the growth of new tissue to replace damaged tissue

sexual reproduction a form of reproduction involving two parents and the union of germ cells (sperm and egg)

somatic cell a cell other than a germ cell

stem cell a primitive type of cell found in embryos and some body tissues that is capable of becoming many different types of specialized cells

tissue culture the growth of tissue outside the body

totipotent capable of becoming any type of cell

vector a microscopic vehicle used to transfer DNA from one organism to another

63